BOOKS BY JOHN GASPARD

The Como Lake Players Mysteries
ACTING CAN BE MURDER
DYING TO AUDITION
REHEARSED TO DEATH

The Eli Marks Mystery Series
THE AMBITIOUS CARD (#1)
THE BULLET CATCH (#2)
THE MISER'S DREAM (#3)
THE LINKING RINGS (#4)
THE FLOATING LIGHT BULB (#5)
THE ZOMBIE BALL (#6)
THE MAGIC SQUARE (#7)
THE SELF-WORKING TRICK (#8)

Stand-Alone Novels
THE SWORD & MR. STONE
A CHRISTMAS CARL
THE GREYHOUND OF THE BASKERVILLES
THE RIPPEROLOGISTS

Filmmaking Books
FAST, CHEAP AND UNDER CONTROL
FAST, CHEAP AND WRITTEN THAT WAY
TELL THEM IT'S A DREAM SEQUENCE
WOMEN MAKE MOVIES

"TELL THEM IT'S A DREAM SEQUENCE."

AND OTHER SMART ADVICE FROM TOP FILMMAKERS

JOHN GASPARD

Published by Albert's Bridge Books

Minneapolis, MN 55419

Manufactured in the United Sates of America

Library of Congress Cataloging-in-Publication Data

Gaspard, John, 1958-

Tell Them It's A Dream Sequence And Other Smart Advice From Top Filmmakers / John Gaspard

1. Motion Picture authorship. 2. Low budget motion pictures. 3. Filmmakers-- Interview. I. Title

Thanks to the two Amys

Amy Gaspard for putting up with yet another book.

And Amy Oriani for also putting up with yet another book. And proofreading the damned thing as well.

INTRODUCTION

This book may not change your life, but it will most likely change the way you make your next movie ... which could in turn, I suppose, change your life.

The genesis of this book was a conversation I had with Lance Weiler and Stefan Avalos, two bright guys who made a very interesting (and very successful) little fake documentary called *The Last Broadcast*.

During the course of our rambling conversation, Stefan said something that I'd been encountering for years:

> *"I'm amazed," Stefan said, "how filmmakers always re-invent the wheel every time they make a project. They make the same mistakes that every filmmaker before them has made. That's the downside to the independent spirit -- people are fiercely independent. 'Don't you tell me ... that I'm headed right for the edge of a cliff.' "*

This book is designed to help you long before you reach the edge of that cliff.

In this book I've assembled 37 key ideas and smart advice gleaned from interviews with some of the most successful and talented filmmakers working today. In addition to their primary ideas, you'll also come across a variety of smaller thoughts that may come in handy.

For the sake of clarity, I've divided the ideas into five categories that roughly track the course a filmmaker follows as she or he attempts to make their feature.

However, in reality, the book can be read in any order. Pick it up, flip to any page, and you're likely to find a piece of advice that you can use, or that you may wish you *had* used on your last project.

The key to getting the most out of this book is to look at each idea and ask yourself (in the words of my friend, business consultant Joe Calloway), "What's _my_ version of this?" How can this idea – in its present form or in an adapted manifestation – help me make a better film and make me a better filmmaker?

So glance through the book when you have a few spare moments. Pick it up before you begin your next project. Refer to it for inspiration while you're up to your neck in problems on your current project.

Or pass it along to another filmmaker who's headed, like the indomitable Wile E. Coyote, toward a cliff of their own.

PART I
GETTING STARTED

"I just took a leap."

Film editor Amy Holden Jones kicked off her directing career with "Slumber Party Massacre." She went on to write the hits "Mystic Pizza," "Indecent Proposal" and "Beethoven."

How did *Slumber Party Massacre* come about?

AMY HOLDEN JONES: I had come out of documentary films and couldn't make a living in them. I had won the AFI student film festival with a documentary. Martin Scorsese was one of the judges of that festival, and he used me as his assistant on *Taxi Driver* and then introduced me to Corman.

I had no money and I had to make a living, so I became a film editor. I worked for a while as a film editor and was beginning to get successful at it. I realized that if I keep this up, I'm going to be typed as a film editor. I did several smaller movies, one for MGM and a small Hal Ashby movie, and I was going to do *E.T.* for Spielberg. I thought, 'I'll be a film editor unless I make a movie,' so I went back to Roger Corman, who I had edited a film for when I was 22 years old.

So I went back and said, "What would I have to do to be a director?" And Roger looked at the documentary, and it didn't show him enough about what he wanted, because it was an art documentary in a way. He said, "You have to show me that you can do what I do."

I had never written anything, so I was looking for an existing script. I went into his library of scripts, scripts that he hadn't made, and I took several of them. I read one called *Don't Open the Door*. And it had a prologue that was about eight pages long. It had a dialogue scene, a suspense scene and an action scene.

My husband was a cinematographer. My neighbor was a soundman. We borrowed some lights, used our own house. I did the special effects, and I got UCLA theater students to act in it.

We spent three days and shot those first eight pages. Then I put them together at night on Joe Dante's system - he was doing *The Howling*. I would work at night, after hours, on his Movieola and he gave me some temp music cues.

Then I dropped off this nine-minute reel for Roger that had a dialogue scene, a suspense scene and an action/horror scene, to show him that I could do those three different kinds of things which make up an exploitation movie.

He called me up and had me come in and asked me how much it had cost me to do it. And I said it cost about $2,000, which is what it had cost. He said, "You have a future in the business," and asked me how much I would need to direct the rest of the script. The truth was, I had never read the rest of the script, all I had read was the first eight pages. So I just, out of the air, said "$200,000." And he said, "Let's do it, you're directing this movie."

I just took a leap. I called Spielberg and told him the situation and he was kind enough to release me from editing *E.T.* I rewrote *Slumber Party Massacre* in about four weeks as I cast it. And, indeed, we made it for $200,000.

CHRIS KENTIS ON "OPEN WATER"

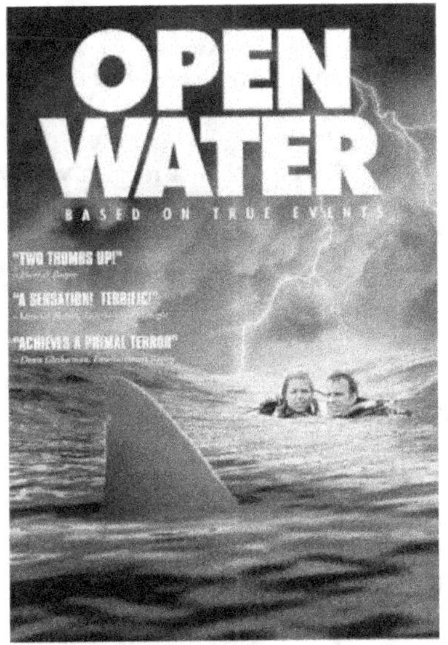

"Find your voice. Stick to your vision."

Chris Kentis and his wife financed "Open Water" themselves, traveling to the Bahamas on weekends to shoot this classic suspense film with a cast of unknowns.

What was your biggest goal on this movie?

CHRIS KENTIS: On this film, the idea was to really try to find our voice. To anyone trying to start out and make a film, it's critical to find your voice. Not that that's an easy thing to get in touch with, but that's what this film was about.

Why is that important?

CHRIS KENTIS: Because there are so many talented people out there making movies. All you really have to offer is your own point of view. I think when you start out making movies, you can't help but want to copy what you've seen before.

And so this project was about the process. When the film was first done, before we got to any festivals -- and we got rejected from plenty of festivals -- I remember screening the film for the actors.

They were thrilled with the film, and I said, "Let's remember this feeling. We're done, we're successful. This movie might not ever make it anywhere, no one might ever see it but us and our parents. But we did what we set out to do."

We were really proud and it felt really good, and none of us had any regrets.

So you never anticipated the success the film would have?

CHRIS KENTIS: It certainly wasn't realistic to ever expect what was going to happen from that point on, and we're thrilled that it did.

What was the best decision you made on *Open Water*?

CHRIS KENTIS: The best decision was to not try to second-guess what an audience was going like, because there was no guessing that anyway -- Hollywood's still trying to figure that out. To stick to our guns, to stick to our vision.

It's really hard work, and it took a long time, but it's a really, really good way to spend a couple of years. It's time really well spent.

JOHN MCNAUGHTON ON "HENRY: PORTRAIT OF A SERIAL KILLER"

"Redefine the genre."

When John McNaughton was given $100,000 and the directive to create a horror film, he looked at the competition and decided the only way to win was to re-write the rules. He went on to direct "Mad Dog and Glory" and "Wild Things."

Did you set out to make such a controversial movie?

JOHN MCNAUGHTON: I intended to make something very shocking. I remember, in my youth, pictures that sort of crossed the line. Back in those days, there would be these incredibly lurid radio advertisements that if you listened to rock music on the radio a lot -- like most kids in my generation did -- they had these incredibly lurid campaigns for pictures like *Last House on the Left* and *Night of the Living Dead* and *Texas Chainsaw Massacre*.

Those pictures were sort of watersheds, alongside pictures like *The Wild Bunch*. *The Wild Bunch* was incredibly shocking; up until then, in a Western, if somebody got shot they fell down. There was no squib work, there was no spouting blood.

If was like, "Okay, you've got $100,000 and a chance to do a film and it's going to have to be a horror film, so let's make a horror film that is going to horrify." (Co-writer) Richard Fire and I set ourselves a goal, and it was if we're charged with a horror film, a. Let's redefine the genre, and b., Totally horrify the audience.

Like many things, the words "horror film" is like "liberal and conservative." The original meanings of the words have gotten lost. One would think that conservatives would be interested in conserving the environment, because the word comes from conservation.

When you think of "horror film" now, it's a set of conventions and we meant to defy those conventions: Monsters, creatures from outer space, ghosts, and the genre often includes the super-natural or something beyond reality.

But we didn't have a budget for any of that, so we set ourselves the goal of, "How can we most completely horrify an audience without using the traditional conventions?"

PART II
THE SCRIPT

ERIC BOGOSIAN ON "SUBURBIA"

"I always begin with a theme."

Eric Bogosian's play "subUrbia," about a group of young people hanging out in a mini-mart parking lot, was made into a film by "Slacker" writer-director, Richard Linklater.

When you write, do you begin with story, character or theme?

ERIC BOGOSIAN: I begin with character and theme. The theme dances around in my head, almost like an editing device as I put my characters in motion with a story. But before anything, I think of the people who will populate my stage.

In the case of *subUrbia*, I began with five student actors in workshop playing the characters. I had them simply hanging out and discussing a variety of topics. There was no plot to speak of in the first set of pages.

How did you create the characters?

ERIC BOGOSIAN: The characters are there within me. They are the archetypes I "need" to conceptualize my inner world. In the case of subUrbia, the cast of characters derived almost directly from the cast of characters who, in my mind, represent my friends from my high school days.

How important is having a theme before you start to write?

ERIC BOGOSIAN: I always begin with a theme. It usually morphs as I'm writing but in the long run, the theme must have importance for me in the present, as I'm writing. I need the theme to do my writing, but I don't mind if the audience doesn't see the theme or misunderstands what the theme is.

In the case of *subUrbia* I don't think many people "got" the theme as I originally conceived it. (And what is that? you might ask. My answer is: Too complicated to explain, that's why I write plays. If I wrote themes, I would be a scholar and write theses.)

DYLAN KIDD ON "ROGER DODGER"

"Your unconscious is trying to tell you what the movie wants to be."

Dylan Kidd's "Roger Dodger" stars Campbell Scott as a smooth-talking ladies' man who schools his young nephew about sex and women during a surprise visit to New York.

Where did the idea for the story come from?

DYLAN KIDD: It started with the idea of a guy who feels like he can tell everyone else what they're thinking. It was based on a friend of mine, who in college had this strange ability to go up strangers and take their psychology apart in minute detail. It struck me as disturbing but also very compelling.

I started with Roger. It ended up being a buddy movie, but his nephew didn't come in until later drafts. You go through a certain amount of time thinking, "Well, maybe this guy is compelling enough, maybe people will sit and watch a train wreck for an hour and a half."

And then there was a point where I realized there has to be some foil, a character who we want to protect has to enter the movie, there has to be a reason for people to hang on and keep watching.

So your first draft was really just the starting point for you, right?

DYLAN KIDD: For me, it's really important that the first draft be the spill draft. I'm the exact opposite of someone who knows the ending before they begin. For me, the first draft is the spill-it draft. And after that you can look at it and think, "Well, I have a 70-page first act, that probably can't work."

But your first time through is when your unconscious is really trying to tell you what the movie wants to be. Maybe what the movie wants to be is that the first act is the entire movie, and that's the lesson, as opposed to, "Oh, I need to shorten the act." Maybe it's, "Oh, I need to lose the second and third act."

For me it's important to follow your bliss in that first draft, even if it ends up at 180 pages or you hate everything but ten percent of it. At least you've got that ten percent, which is ten more than a lot of people have.

ALI SELIM ON "SWEET LAND"

"Always write in active voice."

Successful commercial director Ali Selim spent thirteen years getting his first feature, "Sweet Land," from the page to the screen.

What do you think is the best advice you've ever gotten about writing?

ALI SELIM: Oddly, it's not that profound, but I carry it with me. It's about screen direction and it's this: always write in active voice, not passive voice. I had one draft that was entirely in the passive voice and I didn't even know what that meant, even though I was an English major. I was like, "what are you talking about?"

It amounted to changing "Olaf is sitting" to "Olaf sits" and "Olaf is harvesting" to "Olaf harvests." I did that on EVERY LINE of screen direction throughout the entire script.

In doing so, the script went from this "distant, over there, who are they?" story to an immediate and present emotion. The subconscious somehow took over and suddenly actors were saying, "I have to do this film."

It was weird. Prior to that they called it "soft." When I made it active they called it "lean and athletic." No scene changes. No new behaviors. No sex scenes or car crashes. Just drop the "ing" and add an "s." Go figure.

But while it was a lightning bolt for me, it is probably a "duh!" for most writers.

Screen direction should almost always be about behavior. I think a lot of poorly-written scripts make it about movement -- moving left, moving right, moving towards the window, moving away from the window -- and sometimes that's important for blocking. But it's not as important to an actor as behavior.

Keep it in the active voice and concentrate on behavior.

WHIT STILLMAN ON "METROPOLITAN"

"People are interested in hearing a story."

Whit Stillman was nominated for an Academy Award for writing his witty, class-conscious low-budget screenplay "Metropolitan," which introduced the audience to the first of his hyper-verbal characters.

How was the process of writing the screenplay for *Metropolitan* different from how you work now on studio projects?

WHIT STILLMAN: I think it was good writing a film that wasn't in the development process, because I'm not sure it's very helpful having a lot of voices in on the creation of a script. I think they try to smooth things and homogenize things and explain things. It's better making it a kind of goofy voyage and ride, when you have to just be honest with yourself about what you're doing and where your mistakes are and what isn't working.

On *Metropolitan*, I found the least helpful comments were from people who thought they were in the film business. Unsuccessful screenwriter friends, who were very, very critical of certain things, while my sociology professor/godfather was very, very supportive and loved the things that the screenwriter friends said were breaking the rules.

Do you remember what their criticisms were?

WHIT STILLMAN: I remember I had this long monologue that the Chris Eigeman character recites about this girl, Polly Perkins. It went on for pages and pages. My screenwriter friend was indignant about how terrible that was and my sociology professor/godfather thought it was a wonderful story.

What I found when we shot the film was that there were long speeches that didn't work, but they were the sociological speeches by the Charlie character, played by Taylor Nichols. If it was a very long sociological speech, we really had to fight hard to whittle those down and make them pertinent, while the long narrative about Polly Perkins, although it's just one guy talking, actually works perfectly fine.

It's a story. People are interested in hearing a story. And film is so wonderful in the sense that you can have people's reaction.

DAN FUTTERMAN ON "CAPOTE"

"There is a moral debt."

Dan Futterman was nominated for an Academy Award for this, his first screenplay, which examined the relationship between writer Truman Capote and killer Perry Smith while Capote was writing the classic "In Cold Blood."

What were the upside and the downside of writing about a real person?

DAN FUTTERMAN: I always hated that moment in school when the teacher, I think inevitably a somewhat lazy teacher, would give the assignment, "Write a story about whatever you want," and I would just panic. My mind would just be a complete blank. But if I got a very specific assignment to write "Why does this character have to confront this thing in this story in Chapter Three," then I was off and running.

Rules are good for me. In that way, I think writing about a real person, knowing basically what the rules are -- you can take a little bit of license, but try to stick to the facts as much as humanly possible -- that felt liberating to me. It has a way of focusing my imagination, I guess, instead of feeling like anything goes and then I'm screwed.

I recently have had correspondence with Wallace Shawn, who is William Shawn's son. He and his brother are not terribly happy about the way William Shawn is portrayed in the film.

I knew that Capote had three different editors involved in the book. One was William Shawn of *The New Yorker*, one was Bennett Cerf at Random House, and then when Cerf retired, a guy named Joe Fox took over. That just seemed too confusing to present in a movie. We needed one editor and I choose that to be William Shawn, and he would do everything that all the other guys did as well. That upset Wallace and I feel badly about it. If I were able to go back, I would try to solve it.

What you encounter is that, even if the people have died, there is a moral debt owed to them in terms of trying to adhere as strictly as possible to the truth. It's something I tried to be very conscious of, but in this particular case, I think I came up short.

It didn't occur to me at the time that any of the things I had him doing could possibly be upsetting to anybody, but that was my own take and I see now why his sons are upset. Looking back now, I would try to find a way to fix it.

JON FAVREAU ON "SWINGERS"

"It's that emotional connection."

Screenwriter-actor Jon Favreau and Vince Vaughn became breakout stars in this low-budget hit about LA hipsters. Favreau went on to direct "Elf" and "Iron Man."

Was *Swingers* based on your life?

JON FAVREAU: It wasn't a true story, but it was definitely based on people and places and inspired by events that I had experienced.

When you write from that, you're incorporating a lot of things that are very real and well understood by you. And the script inherits a certain sincerity and a certain subconscious vision that you might not even be aware of when you're doing your first script, if it's a personal one. It becomes much more difficult later on to do that.

But if you stick to things that you know and understand and people that you know, it allows a very true voice and you tend to come off as a better writer than really are, because you're incorporating so much of reality into your piece.

When did you realize how much fun audiences would have with the phone message scene?

JON FAVREAU: Not on the set. The crew was not very entertained by it. We shot all the apartment stuff in a day and a half, so about a quarter of the movie was shot in a day and a half on paper. So that was one of those things that was crammed into a very crowded day at that location.

It wasn't until the whole movie was cut together and the significance of that moment, where it fell in the story, it was definitely a pivotal point in the film.

And because you were so emotionally involved in that moment in the movie, the audience was engaged with the film. And had they not been engaged with the character, that scene would not have been as funny or as poignant. It was because of the work that had been done by everybody involved up until then that it was funny.

It all goes to emotion. If you're emotionally engaged, everything is going to be funnier, more satisfying, scar-ier, everything.

It's the one thing that you really have going for you in a small movie, that you're doing something that's so real and usually so personal that you have a level of emotional engagement that you will not get in a high-budget, high-concept movie.

MIRANDA JULY ON "ME AND YOU AND EVERYONE WE KNOW"

"Characters have intentions."

Writer and performance artist Miranda July brought her unique sensibility to her first feature, a multi-character movie about relationships and seemingly random connections.

What is your writing process?

MIRANDA JULY: At the very beginning, I just sit down and write dialogue. Writing dialogue was very familiar to me, because I'd been doing that for performances for a long time. Then I act out the characters as I'm writing that dialogue.

But I usually start with some really irrelevant detail, seemingly out of left field. Like, "I know she has a powder compact in this scene."

So I'm starting with that, rather than starting with, "She needs to connect with this man."

There's something about the irrelevance and the physicality of something like that. And often it's humor that gets me into a scene, because I'm enjoying myself when I'm writing something funny. And in enjoying myself, just as hopefully the audience will, you kind of open up and then other stuff can come out, maybe deeper stuff.

So it's never starting with the big idea; it's always something physical or quite often something visual. For example, a little door peephole that a girl can open in the door. Sometimes I'll write a scene and I won't know until later why that little door will be opened. It seems very magical to me, like, "Oh, Richard knocks on the door because he's looking for his son," but I actually already wrote a version with a girl opening a peephole, without any clear objective.

At what point do you start to connect these disparate scenes?

MIRANDA JULY: Pretty quickly there are characters. And characters have intentions, whether you're conscious of it or not and pretty quickly there's a set of problems. So then much of the scenes come out of trying to solve problems. Like, how can the audience be reminded that she's thinking about him? And that becomes the scene with the "Me" and "You" shoes.

There's a certain point where there's just enough stuff where you establish problems. And at that point you start solving problems.

TOM DICILLO ON "LIVING IN OBLIVION"

"Tap into something personal."

Tom DiCillo's feature – about a director driven to the edge while making a low-budget film – is considered to be the definitive movie about making a movie.

How did you come to write the script for *Living In Oblivion*?

TOM DICILLO: It wasn't born out of, "Hey, let me make a funny movie." It really came out of one of the most intense periods of anger and frustration in my career. And, ironically, it turned out to be the funniest movie I've ever made. I think in some way that is part of what makes my humor my humor. It is humor based upon real, human intensity, desperation, foolishness.

One of the things that makes the script so strong is that all the obstacles that you put in Nick's way are real obstacles that you've experienced in that position.

TOM DICILLO: Whatever you write, you have to tap into something personal for yourself. I used to have an acting teacher who said to me, "If it ain't personal, it ain't no good." There's something to be said for that.

Even if you're talking about a character, someone who's not you, you have to find something that is you that you really do believe and that you've really experienced and you have real feelings about, and put it in that character's mouth and in their hearts and minds.

But at the same time, I don't want to ever make it seem like when I write that it's just me. I'm not interested in that.

Even with my first film, *Johnny Suede* -- sure, I put a lot of myself into that character -- but I also was very clearly trying to find a way to make it more objective, more universal, something that other people could relate to.

I absolutely believe that if you can find a way to tap into something that's very personal, and then make a creative leap from there, that's the best way to do it.

Anger by itself is not enough. You have to have the creative imagination coming into play as well.

KELLY MASTERSON ON "BEFORE THE DEVIL KNOWS YOU'RE DEAD"

"Raise the stakes."

Kelly Masterson's "Before the Devil Knows You're Dead" is a classic rags-to-riches screenwriting story: Write a great script and Hollywood will come find you.

What was going on in your writing career before you started *Before the Devil Knows You're Dead?*

KELLY MASTERSON: Nothing. My career was dead in the water. I was working at a bank in Manhattan.

I wrote *Devil* in 1999 and it was my first original screenplay. The script was optioned by a succession of producers but I had lost hope by 2006 after several false starts.

I got a call out of the blue from the producers that the project was a go. They had Sidney Lumet on board to direct. The entire cast was in place – Philip Seymour Hoffman, Albert Finney, Ethan Hawke and Marisa Tomei. I was totally shocked.

I got that call on May 16th and they started shooting on July 10, 2006. I had no time to react. I quit my job at the bank as soon as the money cleared.

What did you learn in the process of writing *Before the Devil Knows You're Dead* that you'll take with you to other projects?

KELLY MASTERSON: Raise the stakes. I don't mean put the hero in more jeopardy or add a ticking clock. I mean dig deeper – make it more personal and more emotionally significant. Get right into the guts of the characters.

While I often try to pull my characters in two or more directions, I think Sidney's contribution took my material into richer psychological territory. This gave the wonderful actors great stuff to work with in which the emotional stakes were very high. When I am working on projects now, I ask myself the question: how do I get further into this character and really rock him?

What advice would you give to screenwriters who are still struggling to get their work seen and (hopefully) produced?

KELLY MASTERSON: Don't give up. I wrote for 20 years before *Devil* got made. And find your voice. I tried for many years to imitate others or to write in "commercial" genres and did not have any success. I wrote *Devil* from some original place within myself and never dreamed it would get made, let alone succeed. Keep at it.

REBECCA MILLER ON "PERSONAL VELOCITY: THREE PORTRAITS"

"Boil your screenplay down to what's most important."

Rebecca Miller adapted her short-story collection, "Personal Velocity," shooting all three stories on digital video for about $150,000.

What's the best advice that you're ever received about writing?

REBECCA MILLER: The best advice I ever received was from a screenwriter named Tom Kohl. He read the first screenplay I ever wrote.

He said, "This is a very personal screenplay, it has your own stamp on it. Don't ever let people, with their advice, sand it down and make it smooth and turn it into something that could have been written by a lot of different people."

People give you a lot of advice, and a lot of that advice is just turning things into something average. Unless that's what you're looking to do; if you're looking to do that, that's fine. But if you're looking to create something that's really your own, then you have to keep what's unusual about it and what's even jarring about it.

One thing I would say, especially for people who are starting out -- this is a big piece of advice that I definitely learned from my first screenplay that was never produced -- is to allow yourself to be humble enough to boil your screenplay down to what's most important in the pool of ideas you have.

In other words, I think when you start out, you tend to try to write about a lot of different things and put a lot of themes into your script. A lot of themes can exist in a piece, in a subterranean way, but that doesn't mean that your story can't be simple.

For example, in *Personal Velocity*, as many things that are going on there, they're three very simple stories. A woman is escaping from an abusive marriage. A woman is propelled out of her own marriage by her ambition. A woman nearly gets killed in an accident and then tries to make sense of that accident by rescuing a hitchhiker. They're simple stories.

When I first started out I wrote a screenplay that was so complicated -- it had everything I had ever thought of in it. There were these two little girls in it, and they were the most real people in the screenplay. And my friend Michael Rohatyn, who is the guy who composes all the music for my movies, said, "Why don't you just write a movie about those two little girls?" And I ended up doing that, and that was *Angela*.

It was such good advice. Sometimes you just take the fingernail off the giant, and the fingernail is your story.

KENNETH LONERGAN ON "YOU CAN COUNT ON ME"

"The rewrite frenzy."

Kenneth Lonergan is a successful playwright who's found the secret of how to balance Hollywood jobs with low-budget, from-the-heart productions. He was nominated for an Academy Award for his screenplay for "You Can Count on Me," which he also directed.

How do you know when a script is done?

KENNETH LONERGAN: It feels right. I always feel that the ending must be at least as good as the rest of the movie. If the ending isn't great, I feel like it's not a successful endeavor. I feel that if I have the right ending than that's a big help. And then I feel that if there's nothing else that I can work on and improve, then I basically leave it alone.

So you don't believe in endless re-writes?

KENNETH LONERGAN: You can always futz around with it, but unfortunately there's a certain point when I start rewriting it that I start making it worse. Thankfully, I think I've learned to identify that point and then I leave it alone.

When you get out of the groove of it, I really think it's dangerous to mess around with it too much.

I tend to rewrite myself a lot as I'm going, but not endlessly. I find that a lot of writers are too ready to rewrite stuff, which is dangerous because they just get lost instantly. I know I do.

New writers are way too eager to take other people's comments and show it to everyone and get all the feedback they can get.

So you're not a big fan of the process of getting notes from committees?

KENNETH LONERGAN: The feeding frenzy in the movie culture now to have everyone dive and anyone give a note, I just find it repellent and very bad for the scripts and for the audience, ultimately.

I think the rewrite frenzy is just appalling. It's shocking; I'm still shocked at 43 at how cavalierly people think it's okay to just chatter away about something someone's worked on for two years and the assumptions behind it.

Personally, if I'm writing a screenplay for somebody else, I would get it to where I think it's good, but I wouldn't go one step beyond that, because I know it's going to be ripped to pieces no matter what.

PART III
PRE-PRODUCTION

HENRY JAGLOM ON "SOMEONE TO LOVE"

"The enemy of art is the absence of limitations."

Henry Jaglom is probably the most independent of all current independent filmmakers. Schooled in the Actors Studio approach, he brings a unique sense of realism and honesty to all of the nearly 20 features he's made.

You're known for not rehearsing before you shoot. What's the benefit of working that way?

HENRY JAGLOM: The magic of reality. The honest surprise of what happens the first time somebody thinks of something or you see them thinking and discovering it and saying it.

God, I would die if I rehearsed and someone in rehearsal gave me a great moment, because a great moment is what you look for in film. It's all about the moment.

The most truthful moments, it seems to me, are the moments that just happen and even surprise the person themselves as they're saying something, because they don't know they're going to be saying it.

If you rehearse, no matter how good you are, you know you're going to be saying it. And unless you've got a Brando or a Meryl Streep or the handful of actors who are better each time, you've got human behavior which is better and truest the first time.

You once told me a great story about something Orson Wells said to you about limitations ...

HENRY JAGLOM: I was complaining about not having more time, not having more money to do something I wanted to do, and Orson said this line that I now have over my editing machine. He said, 'The enemy of art is the absence of limitations.'

That was just about the most important thing that has ever been said to me, because if you don't have limitations you start throwing technology or money at a problem.

But if you have a limitation, you have to find a creative solution, and therefore you create art.

For me the most valuable lesson from Orson, and it happened during that movie, was to make whatever happens work. It's good to have limitations, because you have to find an artistic or creative way to surmount them.

And it's more fun.

WAYNE KRAMER ON "THE COOLER"

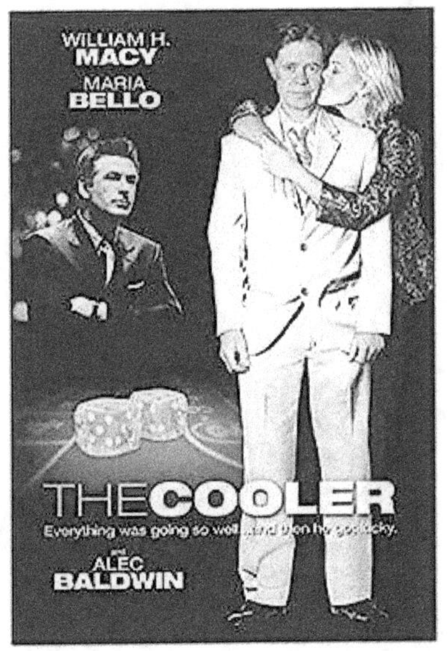

"It's all about collaboration."

Wayne Kramer's "The Cooler" starts with a simple premise (What if a casino cooler – hired to make luck disappear – suddenly falls in love and can no longer cool a table?) – and brings it to life with the stellar William H. Macy in the title role.

Is there a key lesson you took away from your experience on *The Cooler*?

WAYNE KRAMER: For me, I learned that it was all about collaboration. Surround yourself with talented people who understand your vision for the film and let them bring their best to the table.

If your ego gets in the way, you'll only end up hurting yourself.

At the same time, you cannot allow your vision for the film to be usurped by cast or crew. You have to follow your gut and it's a difficult balance to maintain.

Directing is a tough job and everyone around you on the set seems to be having more fun - because you're too busy stressing about the next setup or an actor that you haven't cast yet, or a million different things.

You have to stay focused at all times and be able to think quickly on your feet.

You also have to KNOW your film. If you know your film, you'll be up to the challenge. It's also about keeping the film tonally consistent.

Preparation and collaboration are everything.

And CONFIDENCE. Even if it's an act. Never let them see you sweat.

BOB ODENKIRK ON "MELVIN GOES TO DINNER"

"Having a few name people would help the movie."

Director Bob Odenkirk put the virtually unknown cast of the play "Phyro-Giants!" in the leads for the film version (renamed "Melvin Goes To Dinner"), but then added some name talent in well-placed cameos to help sell the finished film.

Although the cast is relatively unknown, you did add some

cameos by better-known performers. What was your thinking behind that?

BOB ODENKIRK: I knew that we weren't going to use any names in the leads. And I thought just having a few name people would help the movie, and I think it did help.

Now, some of the people, like Jack Black and Melora Walters, wouldn't let us put their name or their image on the poster, which is fine and understandable, and in fact I would agree.

The last thing I would want would be for it to be released as *'The Jack Black Movie.'* People would hate me, Jack, and the asshole who made the poster.

I do think the cameos help. It helps people to consider the movie legitimate. The thing I'm most happy about is that those people were right for their parts, they were funny and good in their parts, and they don't overshadow the movie.

You like Jack Black, and you like Maura Tierney, and you like Melora Walters, they're all good in their roles. David Cross is great.

But none of them overshadows what the movie's about, none of them dislocates the core of the movie.

When the movie's over, you don't go, "Wow, that was about Jack Black's scene." Instead, you totally go, "That was about this couple who are lying and this friend who's in a bad relationship and this girl's story about ghosts," and about the ninth thing you mention is that Jack Black's in it. And that's perfect. Perfect.

JOAN MICKLIN SILVER ON "HESTER STREET"

"Make a part work for the whole."

Director/writer Joan Micklin Silver chose to do a period piece for her first, very low-budget film "Hester Street." This required extra ingenuity to bring historic New York and Ellis Island alive in the film.

Was there anything in the adaptation that you really wished you could have included, but budget prevent-ed it?

JOAN MICKLIN SILVER: There were many, many things. For example, just after we had made the movie, *Godfather II* came out. And in *Godfather II* there's a very long scene on Ellis Island in which there's an overhead traveling shot. The boy who will grow up to be Robert DeNiro is sitting on the bench and you see him in isolation, all by himself.

It's just a stunning shot, and I remember that my husband Ray and I saw it and were just pinching each other's arms in jealousy.

It was one thing after another, just constantly trying to figure out how I could tell the story without having a budget that allowed me to tell the full story, where I could recreate the Lower East Side, like they did in *Godfather II*.

When it came time to do Ellis Island, I had to do what I think just about all low-budget filmmakers do and that is that you make a part work for the whole. You have to ask yourself, "What's the most important thing about this?"

And I decided that it was the separation between the ones who were already there and the ones who had just arrived. Therefore, I thought if I could do some sort of a fence or something that would keep the two groups apart, that would help to say what I wanted to say.

I remember that the fence cost about $800, which was a huge portion of our budget. I think it worked -- it isn't re-creating Ellis Island, which if I'd had a chance, of course I would have done. Those were the sorts of things that we did all the time.

ERIC MENDELSOHN ON "JUDY BERLIN"

"Work with your friends."

Eric Mendelsohn learned an important lesson on his first feature, "Judy Berlin." Surround yourself with people who want you to succeed.

What did you learn from previous films that you vowed not to repeat on *Judy Berlin*?

ERIC MENDELSOHN: I had this crazy idea at the beginning of my short, *Through an Open Window*. I thought I'm going to try to make this everyone's film.

What did you mean by that?

ERIC MENDELSOHN: It meant that the grips are going to feel involved and the craft services person is going to feel involved and passionate and want to work on it because I'm going to include everyone.

And that was a terrible decision. And I learned on the short film never to do it again.

Why was it a terrible decision?

ERIC MENDELSOHN: It's a terrible decision because films aren't democracies. They're monarchies. And the guy or the woman who's a grip on your film isn't going to go to a festival with you, isn't going to win an award with you.

They're going to go on to a new job and be a grip again. They do not, and cannot, be expected to have the same passionate involvement as you do. They shouldn't. They should have professionalism.

Hence, if you work with your friends, they can be expected to have a level of passion above and beyond a paycheck. They have an active interest in your success and the success of the project.

And you can't buy that. You can't go on-line and rustle up a crew with that. You can't put an ad in the paper and get that.

Those people who are there with you who are your friends have a vested interest that is just priceless.

STEVEN SODERBERGH ON "SEX, LIES & VIDEOTAPE"

"Keep your prejudices in check."

In his first feature, "sex, lies & videotape," Steven Soderbergh learned an important lesson about keeping an open mind through all parts of the film-making process.

How did you approach the casting of this film?

STEVEN SODERBERGH: I think you have an idea, and you stick with that idea until you're confronted with the fact that there's something better than your idea. I think the smart play is to go with the better idea.

In the case of casting Andie MacDowell in *sex, lies & videotape*, I was laboring under the illusion that she was not much more than a model and couldn't deliver what was required. Fortunately for me, she came in and proved me wrong. And I was happy to be proven wrong.

It happened to me the other day on a movie we're starting next month. It's a supporting role, and one of the people who came in was someone I know and who, on first blush, I would have said, "No, I don't think he's really right for this."

Of all the people I was looking at, he was the one I would have potentially said, "I know him and I think he's good, I just don't think he's right for this." Sure enough, when I sat down and looked at what he did, I immediately said, "Oh, that's the guy."

What was it that made the difference?

STEVEN SODERBERGH: He did something that was different from what I'd seen him do, and different from what other people were choosing to do, and suddenly he seemed like the only guy who should be doing it. So you have to keep your prejudices in check.

I'm a big believer that you get the cast you're supposed to get. I've had people drop out, many, many, many times, and always, in retrospect, I felt they dropped out because I was supposed to get somebody better. That's just the way it works.

LANCE WEILER AND STEFAN AVALOS ON "THE LAST BROADCAST"

"It's the details that convince people."

Making movies is all about creating a real world for the audience. Weiler and Avalos discovered that reality can be found in the minor details and doesn't have to break your budget.

It's amazing that, even to this day, there are people on the Internet who insist that the events in your movie really happened.

LANCE WEILER: I think a lot of time it's the details that convince people. There were things that would happen that helped, almost accidents. Everyone brought different things at different times; like the way Tony (playing a cop) put ATF on his shirt that day.

STEFAN AVALOS: We call it Theater of the Minimal. The psychologist is a friend of ours who does high-end carpentry. But we brought in some psychology books, just a couple little things here and there --

LANCE WEILER: And that birdhouse.

STEFAN AVALOS: Yes, the cuckoo clock birdhouse. It's amazing how little it takes to convince people. Which is something we were commenting on in the movie: What's reality, what do you believe? And I found it amazing how readily people believed the movie, based on just a couple little pseudo-realities within the movie. I think that perturbed a lot of documentary filmmakers.

LANCE WEILER: When you're working with no money, you look to those locations that you know that you can get that are interesting and that are almost dressed already. Then you just accent them with a couple things here and there, in a very minimalist way, so it's not costing you anything. We took a lot of time to try and find the right places. We looked for places that provided larger production values that didn't cost us anything.

Not having any money made us be more creative. I think sometimes there's a tendency to fall back on money as an answer to a problem, where we found ourselves brainstorming and trying to find ways to make things work without the money.

STEFAN AVALOS: Having no money and really spending no money gave us a carefree attitude that I've never had before or since making movies. We didn't have a producer breathing down our necks concerned about a budget that was spiraling out of control. It's ironic that no having money gave us that freedom.

LANCE WEILER: I remember the shock when we totaled up the receipts, to see the budget at the end. We rounded up, but it was very close, maybe within 28 cents, of $900. And that was the first time we really knew what we had spent.

STEFAN AVALOS: We had wanted to make a movie for no money, but we missed the mark by 900 bucks.

ROGER CORMAN ON "CAGED HEAT"

"Work with your actors in advance."

Clearly Roger Corman knows how to get every penny out of each dollar spent on a movie. This simple lesson — make sure you and the actors agree on the characters before you shoot — is the kind of advice he provided that helped make the careers of directors like Jonathan Demme.

How did you meet Jonathan Demme?

ROGER CORMAN: Jonathan was working out of England, writing publicity for United Artists. I did a film in Ireland for United Artists, and he came over on behalf of UA. It was clear he was a very intelligent young man. He said he was writing publicity but was interested in writing screenplays.

I told him a couple ideas I had and I said, 'If you ever write anything on this, let me know.' He and his partner, Joe Viola, wrote a script and Jonathan produced and directed. They did one more for me, and then they did *Caged Heat*, on which Jonathan made his debut as a director.

You're legendary for taking new directors to lunch and sort of giving them a quick, one-hour course in filmmaking. What are the key messages you impart?

ROGER CORMAN: The most important thing that I point out over and over is preparation. On a ten-day shoot, or a 20-day shoot, you don't have time to create from scratch on the set. As a matter of fact, I don't think you should do that anyway.

My number one rule is to work with your actors in advance, so you and the actors are agreed on at least the broad outline of the performance. Then to have sketched out, if not all of your shots, most of your shots, so you have a shot plan in advance.

Sometimes the plan doesn't work and you have to change it, and sometimes you get a better idea. There will always be shading and nuance with the actors, which will occur in rehearsal on the set before shooting, but you at least have the broad strokes worked out, so you're working on detail work on the set and you can come in and shoot, rather than come in and discuss what you're going to shoot.

Be flexible. Even though you've done all your preparation, don't stick absolutely to the preparation if it doesn't seem to be working. Know that you've got the preparation, but situations change, so be prepared to change with the situations.

PART IV
PRODUCTION

DAN O'BANNON ON "DARK STAR"

"A director doesn't make a movie."

While they were USC students, John Carpenter and Dan O'Bannon created "Dark Star," a Kafka-esque comedy about a spaceship on a mission to destroy unstable suns and the toll the long-term mission takes on the equally unstable crew. O'Bannon went on to write "Alien" and write and direct "Return of the Living Dead."

What's the biggest lesson you took away from *Dark Star*?

DAN O'BANNON: I learned all the wrong lessons on *Dark Star*.

When I finally directed a movie for real, I thought I was supposed to do everything. And I ended up making everybody mad.

I was over-prepared for directing and I was mis-directed by having gone to film school, and thought that the director was supposed to be an auteur and do everything himself.

When I actually tried doing that in a real movie, I found that I couldn't get anything I wanted, because they would sabotage me.

It basically took me two pictures to learn an entirely different orientation toward directing.

What I learned was very simple: A director doesn't make a movie. Everybody else makes the movie.

That means the director doesn't have to know how to do anything.

All the director has to do is be there and stand there and make creative decisions if he feels like it.

I had to swivel around 180 degrees and stop worrying about exactly how I wanted to get everything on the screen and start worrying about how to trick 300 people into doing it for me.

ROGER NYGARD ON "SUCKERS"

"Part of the excitement of filmmaking is taking chances."

Director Roger Nygard moves easily between directing documentaries ("Trekkies"), features ("Suckers") and directing and editing television shows ("The Office," "Curb Your Enthusiasm").

How did you come up with the idea of setting the story on four consecutive Saturdays?

ROGER NYGARD: That was because that's how the car business runs. Every Saturday there's a sales meeting. It's an inspirational meeting, a motivational meeting. It's a time for everybody to gauge where they are against everyone else, because there's always that competitive aspect.

So that's how we broke it down, because the industry that we were writing about breaks itself down monthly and weekly.

How nervous were you about setting the whole first act in that first sales meeting?

ROGER NYGARD: You know, we broke a lot of structural rules with *Suckers*. And, in hindsight, there is a lot I would do differently, having learned what I've learned since then and having seen how that experiment worked, where it worked and where it failed.

Part of the excitement of filmmaking is taking chances sometimes. Sometimes you're going to fail spectacularly. And we took a big chance structuring the first act that way. But I don't think it was the biggest chance we took.

What was the biggest chance?

ROGER NYGARD: The biggest chance in the script was doing a genre shift from the second to the third act, which many people found disconcerting. Audiences are not used to -- and don't like -- when you shift from one genre to another in a movie.

Quentin Tarantino did it also in *From Dusk 'Til Dawn*. It starts out as kind of a crime caper/road chase, and then shifts into a monster movie, which threw a lot of people.

I think that film was less successful than it might have been also, because people just don't like genre shifts. They want to know what the genre is from the beginning of the movie, what's the level of reality of the story, and then you have to stick to it.

If you don't, then you're taking a chance or doing an art film.

JIM MCBRIDE AND L.M. KIT CARSON ON "DAVID HOLZMAN'S DIARY"

"Keep that instant alive."

"David Holzman's Diary" was the first – and some would argue, the best – fake documentary ever made. It follows a few days in the life of David Holzman (L.M. Kit Carson) as he deals, not too successfully, with losing his job, his girlfriend, and finding that his number has come up for the draft.

How did you and Kit write the film?

JIM MCBRIDE: For those parts of the film that took place in his apartment--we really did it all in one long weekend, I think--we spent several days beforehand with just a tape recorder in a room.

I would give him a sense of what I wanted to have happen in a given scene, and then he would put it into his own words, and then we'd listen to the tape and I'd say "I like this, I don't like that, change this."

It was very much controlled improvisation, and by the time we actually went to shoot the scene--although it wasn't written down--we all knew exactly what was going to happen.

Because we didn't have a lot of film to fuck around with, we had to get it on the first or second take. So it was pretty carefully rehearsed.

KIT CARSON: And then when we would shoot, I told Jim that I was not going to rehearse. "Just turn the camera on and I'm going to do it." Because I didn't want to filter the improvisation any further.

If I had rehearsed it before we turned the camera on, it would have turned it into self-conscious thought. And I wanted to keep it raw.

We were satisfied that we had the shape of the scene, built off of the 12-page outline. We knew the beginning, middle and end. But I said to Jim, "I want to surprise you." I had no idea what I was saying when I said that, but the idea was to keep that instant alive, the instant when anything can happen.

I like the idea of not filtering the moment, not knowing what I'm going to do.

JONATHAN LYNN ON "MY COUSIN VINNY"

"I don't really like the camera to be noticed."

British writer and director Jonathan Lynn might have seemed like an unlikely choice to helm this very American comedy. But his British sensibilities and focus on getting the most out of the comedic situation proved that he was the man for the job.

What was it that drew you to the material?

JONATHAN LYNN: I was immediately drawn to it. I have a degree in law, and had always loved courtroom dramas. Among my favorite films are *Anatomy of a Murder*, *The Verdict* and *To Kill A Mockingbird*.

Originality is rare. I had seen plenty of courtroom dramas, and plenty of funny scenes in courtrooms, but I'd never seen what could truly be described as a courtroom comedy, so this seemed to be a great opportunity.

How would you define the visual style for the film?

JONATHAN LYNN: My visual style? I never know how to answer that sort of question. I don't really like the camera to be noticed at all, unless there's a very special reason for it. I want the audience to be totally involved in the characters and their situation.

The biggest challenge was that a large amount of the film takes place in one room, the courtroom. In order for the film not to become visually repetitive or boring, I constantly changed the basic point of view from scene to scene - sometimes shooting from the jury's side, sometimes from opposite the jury, sometimes from behind the judge, sometimes from the spectators' POV.

Within that basic POV, of course, many other camera positions were employed. This meant building a courtroom set, so that walls could be removed when necessary.

I used handheld sometimes, to give a more documentary feel (the whole arrest sequence, for instance, and in the prison bus).

I tried to keep the camera moving, to maintain visual interest and to show the surroundings but, unless the camera was moving with the actors (like on a "walk-and-talk"), I avoided camera movement on big laugh lines - so as not to distract from the actors.

ROGER CORMAN ON "TARGETS"

"All rules are made to be broken."

Although Corman was a strict taskmaster with his directors (no one dared to go over-time or over-budget), he was also a realist and recognized that sometimes you had to bend the rules to get the job done. First-time director Peter Bogdanovich (who went on to direct "The Last Picture Show,"

"Paper Moon" and "What's Up, Doc") proved that point expertly in his first directorial effort, "Targets."

How did you come to produce *Targets*?

ROGER CORMAN: As a result of various complications in a contract, Boris Karloff owed me several days' work. So I wanted to do a horror film, starring Boris Karloff, in which he would only work for those days.

Peter Bogdanovich had been my assistant. I said, "Here's the problem: The picture must star Boris Karloff, but he can only work for these days."

And Peter came up with the idea of Boris as an actor doing a traditional horror film, and in that way we could take some footage out of some of the horror films that Boris had done for me before, and also cut away and tell a parallel story.

The film has a couple of really long, continuous takes, which seem to go against your rule of getting proper coverage.

ROGER CORMAN: It goes a little bit against my rules, but on the other hand, all rules are made to be broken. I do like to get coverage, to get as much coverage as possible.

Yet, at the same time, when you're on a very tight schedule, sometimes you have to sacrifice coverage. And when you do that, sometimes you can make a virtue out of necessity.

ALAN CUMMING ON "THE ANNIVERSARY PARTY"

"Treat people respectfully."

Actors Alan Cumming and Jennifer Jason Leigh met while performing in the Broadway re-mounting of the musical "Cabaret." They decided they liked working together and came up with a digital film project ("The Anniversary Party") that they wrote, directed and starred in together.

How did you divide up chores of writing and directing?

ALAN CUMMING: We didn't, really. People understand the notion that you can write together. I think people have more trouble with the idea of directing together. But it wasn't divided up; it was quite smooth. We both would talk. I would do most of the shouting and general announcements.

But there were certain actors where we said, "You talk to him," or, "I'll talk to her." We were very aware that we get better results with one of us talking to someone rather than the other.

It's not difficult to direct with someone else; it's actually really nice. It was very sort of democratic, with the crew and everyone. There were no trailers. We all ate together. If someone wasn't working, they'd just lie on the lawn.

We tried to open up, ask people's opinions. It's easy to make people feel good about coming to work. You just have to make them feel involved and that you respect their opinion and it's not an autocracy. When you have that attitude, it makes it very easy to have two directors.

What was the biggest lesson you took away from the experience?

ALAN CUMMING: Biggest lesson; Treat people respectfully. There's a sort of vogue, and there has been for decades now, that the director is god and the director is all-knowing.

But when you say to someone, "I don't understand this and I'm asking your advice because you're better at it than me," by doing that and involving people and making the film truly a collaborative process, you get much better results. You get a better film and you get happier people and get an atmosphere on the set that is truly creative.

GRIFFIN DUNNE ON "LISA PICARD IS FAMOUS"

"Be open to accidents and disasters."

In this faux documentary about actors struggling in New York, director Griffin Dunne ("Practical Magic," "Fierce People") discovered that the best way to get great results was to let reality intrude at every point in the process.

How did making this movie differ from your past experiences?

GRIFFIN DUNNE: With movies I'd done before, everything was about preparation, so that there would be absolutely no mistakes, because mistakes would cost so much time and so much money. So you plan everything, if you're really doing your job right, so you're not going to be felled by weather or any of the billions of things that can go wrong. You try to plug every hole before anything sets in.

With this movie, I approached it, before I started shooting, that it was about the lack of preparation and being open to accidents and disasters. It was so small that I thought this would be the fun thing to explore.

So, if she's running to catch the train and she accidentally catches the train and I don't want her to catch the train, then we shoot her catching the train. If she doesn't catch the train, then we shoot that.

Coming from larger budget pictures, did you have any concerns about working with such a small budget?

GRIFFIN DUNNE: I wasn't daunted by how little money I had; I decided to make that part of the style. However, I didn't have that First Feature pressure where I felt I had a lot riding on it.

For me, it was always an experiment and to have a lot of fun and rope in friends and call in favors and go to work in the morning and see how the day turns out. I'd been under so much more pressure before that this was just much more enjoyable to me.

A director's job is to be the most prepared, and this was an exercise in leaving a real part of your creative process to being unprepared and open to accidents.

And I was able to keep those "let's see what happens" balls in the air for most of the picture.

HENRY JAGLOM ON "VENICE/VENICE"

"Tell them it's a dream sequence."

Henry Jaglom's long friendship with film giant Orson Welles provides yet another tip for getting your film made your way.

What advice would you give to a filmmaker who wanted to make a movie like yours?

HENRY JAGLOM: It's really simple: Don't do my kind of movie, do your kind of movie. Figure out what your kind of movie is, not my kind of movie. That would be my advice.

And once you've figured out what your kind of movie is, don't let anybody tell you that anything about it is wrong. Don't let anybody diminish your enthusiasm or excitement about it. And insist that you know what you're doing, even if you don't know what you're doing, because you will find out what you're doing as you go along.

When I was shooting my first film, I had a crew and a cameraman that came from *Love Story*. It was during the Vietnam War, I had long hair and white Capezio shoes and I was totally weird to them, so they showed up wearing American Flag pins in their lapels the next day. They were rather hostile toward me.

I was trying to invent my own style. And the crew kept getting more and more irritated. But mainly they said, "It won't cut. You can't shoot that, it won't cut."

And it was driving me crazy. So at lunch I said to Orson Welles, "Everything I try that's different, they tell me it won't cut." And he said, "Tell them it's a dream sequence."

So after lunch, sure enough on the first shot I said, "I'd like the camera to go from here down to here." The DP said, "The camera go from here to here? That can't possibly cut."

I said, "It's a dream sequence."

"Oh, a dream sequence! How about this?" And he got down on his back on the floor and said, "Look, I could shoot it up against the sky ..." And I said, "Great, great."

I went to Orson that night and said, "I don't understand, why did this change everything?"

He said, "Most people think life has rules. The only place in their life where they know there are no rules, no order, no structure, is in their dreams. When they dream, they know things jump around, things aren't logical, and they accept that, because that's a dream.

"So if you tell them this is a dream sequence, they are freed from all the conventional requirements or the logical, structured, technologically-adept way of doing things. And the artist in them is suddenly freed."

There's not a single movie since then that I haven't used that on somebody. Even on actors, who say, "I don't understand why this person would do that," and I say, "It's a dream sequence." "Oh! Oh, okay!"

PART V
POST-PRODUCTION & DISTRIBUTION

STUART GORDON ON "RE-ANIMATOR"

"Every single scene should have some tension in it."

Editing the film is the point at which you do the last re-write and find a way to get the most out of every scene. Stage and film director Stuart Gordon recognized that fact while putting together his classic low-budget horror film, "Re-Animator."

Is there anything you brought to the filmmaking process from your work as a theater director?

STUART GORDON: It's funny, one of the things that I always did when I was staging a play was, I would very seldom have characters sit down. People sitting down and talking is, I think, one of the most boring things you can do. I would try to avoid that, because I felt that if you have the character sitting down, then the whole story sits down.

When I was doing theater, one of our patrons was an older woman and she would always bring her husband, who didn't really like theater very much. But she dragged him along to see our plays. He was notorious for falling asleep in the middle of the plays, and sometimes snoring. His name was Lester.

So I was always, in the back of my mind, thinking "We've got to keep Lester awake. We have to have something going on every moment to keep Lester from falling asleep." And I think I'm still trying to keep Lester awake.

Was there anything you learned while working on that script that you took to future writing projects?

STUART GORDON: One of the things was that when you're working on a horror film, every single scene should have some tension in it. That was one of the things we really worked on with *Re-Animator*. You really can't have any scenes with people just sort of sitting around and relaxed. You have to really find the tension in each scene.

There needs to be something scary about every single scene in the film, otherwise you're letting the audience off the hook. What you really want to do is to keep people on the edge of their seats all the way through.

MARK DECENA ON "DOPAMINE"

"Go back in and find the story."

Editing is more than just putting the scenes together in script order. Director Mark Decena learned on his first feature, "Dopamine," that there are actually three films: the film you write, the film you shoot, and ultimately, the film you put together in the editing room.

What was the editing process on *Dopamine*?

MARK DECENA: We were cutting as we were going. The editor was a day or two behind, because we had to send the tapes to Los Angeles to get them down-converted. We saw a full assembly cut about three days after we finished shooting. It was insane.

After the assembly cut was done, we realized we had to go back in and find the story, which is always disheartening. I think as a first-timer you think, "Well, I finished the script, and the script as it's shot is going to be great," and then you realize that the story has to be brought out.

How did you find the story in the editing?

MARK DECENA: We ended up moving things around, opening with more of the flashback stuff between the father and the son and the mother issues, using that throughout as the voice of his conscience.

The opening scene was put into the middle of the film, which sounds really strange to script something and have the opening move to the middle of the movie, but it worked.

What did you learn about filmmaking from that experience?

MARK DECENA: It's important to be open to the storytelling process, which is completely collaborative in filmmaking.

You have to have blind faith that you're going to make it, almost a cunning naiveté. You know you're going to do it, and you don't know enough to know that it's really impossible. You have to be naïve, but you still have to be determined and almost cunning in a way to just know it's going to happen, regardless of all the things that fall in front of you, like money falling out at the last minute and actors dropping out.

You have to be passionate about the material. It's got to be a story that you need to tell. If your wife had back surgery two weeks before the shoot, would you still do it? I had to. I didn't have a choice.

KASI LEMMONS ON "EVE'S BAYOU"

"It's not a painting."

The collaborative process doesn't end after you yell "cut" for the final time. First-time director Kasi Lemmons learned that on "Eve's Bayou," losing a major character and gaining a great lesson at the same time.

Was there anything that you hated to lose while making *Eve's Bayou*?

KASI LEMMONS: There was nothing that I hated to lose until the edit and then I lost something I *hated* to lose. It was extremely painful. It was a character named Tomy. He was a member of the family. It was actually a lot of work to cut him out.

He was a great-uncle who lived in the house. I never explain exactly what's wrong with him, but he's mute. In the director's cut, he's in a wheelchair and he's actually sitting in the room when what happens between Louis and Cisely happens. So he knows the truth but he can't speak.

You did a masterful job of cutting him out of the finished movie.

KASI LEMMONS: He's in the movie, but I would have to freeze frame and point him out to you. There are places where we didn't remove him but you just don't see it, your eye doesn't go there.

What drove the decision to cut this fairly major character out of the movie?

KASI LEMMONS: What drove it was notes from the producer, Mark Amin, who was running Trimark. He *hated* that character and we went back and forth over it. Finally I lost him and it was very painful. My crew made t-shirts with an empty wheelchair that read, "Where's Tomy?"

How do you process notes from producers? In the case of Tomy, you had that note before you started shooting but you didn't make the change until you were in editing.

KASI LEMMONS: You make the perfect movie when you write the script, where the world is your oyster and you're making the perfect movie. And then as pre-production goes along you start getting reality checks. I remember one day my agent said to me, "It's not a painting, Kasi." This was after I had made the film and people were starting to comment on it and I was resisting notes.

It's not a painting. It's really a collaborative medium and it requires an audience. It's not just for me alone. It's not even my money, right? It requires cooperation.

The trick is to cooperate and hear your fellow collaborat-ors without losing your vision. That's the tricky thing and that's something that's a little tricky to learn. Some people don't have to be told. They learn it right away and they always know their boundaries and where their line in the sand is drawn.

CAROL LITTLETON ON "THE BIG CHILL"

"You may have needed that scene to write the script, but you don't need the scene for the movie."

It's a scene that everybody's heard about – the famous final flashback scene in "The Big Chill" – which was shot and never used, denying newcomer Kevin Costner his only scene in the film as the old friend, Alex. Editor

Carol Littleton ("E.T.," "Body Heat," "Grand Canyon") explains how this vital scene never made it off the cutting room floor.

You were there. Why was the scene shot and never used?

CAROL LITTLETON: You could talk to five or six different people who worked on the movie and you'd get several different opinions. But being on the inside of that, the ending that Larry and Barbara Benedek wrote was to have a large flashback at the very end of how all these people were -- the roots of their personalities, the roots of who they were going to be -- were actually evident when they were students.

After I first read the script, we sat down and I said, "I feel very uneasy about this flashback. I just don't think you need it." And Larry with his nasal, West Virginia voice, said, "Carol, I can't believe you said that. You are so wrong. I can't believe it. You are so wrong." So I dropped it. When somebody says you're wrong, you drop it.

When we were shooting it I said, "This looks like a masquerade, with everybody in long hair and beads." And Larry said, "Carol, you are so wrong. The reason I wanted to write this script was because of this idea." And I said, "Yes, Larry, you're absolutely right. It's a wonderful idea. You may have needed that scene to write the script, but you don't need the scene for the movie. At all." "You are so wrong, if you mention this one more time!"

Well, in the editing, we put that flashback everywhere. We took it out of the ending, we put it up front, we put it in the middle, we put it in pieces, we spent a lot of time trying to get the flashback to work.

So we showed it with an audience and the movie still did not work as well as it should. So I said, "Larry, why don't we devise an ending, drop the flashback, have two screenings -- one with the flashback and one without -- and let the audience tell us which one is more effective?"

Well, at the screenings, it was clear that the version without the flashback was better.

And the next day, when Larry came into the cutting room, he said, "God dammit, Carol, I wanted you to take that thing out from the beginning! How many times do I have to tell you I'm right?"

GEORGE ROMERO ON "LAND OF THE DEAD"

"Just keep the essentials."

Film legend George Romero ("Night of the Living Dead," "Dawn of the Dead," "Day of the Dead") faces the same problem that all filmmakers face in the editing room: You've lived with the film for a long time and you need to make sure that you're putting the right pieces together to make the best possible movie.

A lot of people tend to look down on genre films.

GEORGE ROMERO: No kidding.

But, editorially, you still run into the same problems that someone might encounter in a non-genre film -- like knowing when to keep a scene or take it out.

GEORGE ROMERO: I think the hardest thing is to have that eye, and I don't necessarily have it. Sometimes I'll cling to a scene and say, "No, this is too important for the character."

For example, in *Land of the Dead*, I really fought for this one scene where John Leguizamo's character goes into an apartment and he finds a guy who has hung himself and who comes back to life right as John is trying to cut him down.

I fought for that scene; I fought for the money, the extra days to shoot it. And all we had was a day and a half to shoot it. But I tried anyway, because I thought it was important, because it was the only selfless act that John's character did in the film.

And it was the only time that we saw someone who had died without being bitten or infected still come back as a zombie. In the mythology, that's an important point to me. So I thought the scene was very, very important.

As it turns out, we just never executed it very well. The actors weren't good, the stunt guys weren't good, and I wound up in the cutting room saying, "Lose it." And we did.

There's an example of a scene that I thought right down until we were editing the movie, like three weeks before delivery, that I thought was super important and then came to realize that we didn't really need it.

That's the hardest thing: to pick out the stuff that you really don't need. Weed it out, weed out the garden and just keep the essentials.

TOM NOONAN ON "WHAT HAPPENED WAS ..."

"Distribution's the creepiest part of making a movie."

Tom Noonan has worked successfully in Hollywood as an actor and a writer. When he set out to make his first feature, "What Happened Was ...," he encountered the same problem that all filmmakers face: How do you keep from getting screwed by distributors? His answer was, "First, make sure that you're not screwing yourself."

How much did it cost to make the movie?

TOM NOONAN: We shot it for $47,000, and then the processing and the editing and all the equipment and music rights and answer prints and inter-negative came to about $130,000. Of which I've never recovered a dime. I don't even get residuals. I made a bad deal. But it's okay; I loved making the movie and I never thought anybody would ever see it.

What was bad about the deal?

TOM NOONAN: When you sell a film to a distributor, there's a certain aspect of the agreement that's called the assumption agreement. It's where the distributor agrees to assume certain costs involved in the distribution of the film, one of which is the residuals for the actors.

Otherwise, if I sell you the film for $75,000 and I pay the crew and I pay everybody back, and then you go out and sell the film everywhere, the more money you make selling the film, the more money the actors have to get paid as residuals. And, unless the distributor assumes that expense, I end up losing money in the end making the film.

And when we made the agreement, I didn't know that and it was left out of the agreement, or somehow it didn't get signed, so I was left with the bill for the residuals. So besides not making any money, I lost some money on the film, paying myself.

I'd done this for a long time and I'd dealt with producers for a long time, and read contracts for a long time. But distribution's the creepiest part of making a movie, and there are so many ways you can get fucked in distribution. I had someone representing me, it wasn't just me, I had somebody who'd sold a lot of movies and they screwed up a little.

But you're still glad you made the movie?

TOM NOONAN: I kind of had to make the movie. I had all these physical problems that prevented me from doing my Hollywood stuff and forced me to do what I really needed to do. You're not here very long, it's over before you know it, and it's a good idea to do at least one or two things in your life that you feel are from your heart or that you have a passion for. But I can't take much credit for it; I just had to do it.

DAN MYRICK ON "THE BLAIR WITCH PROJECT"

"You have to take it all with a grain of salt."

Few filmmakers could dream of reaching the level of success that Dan Myrick found with his first film, "The Blair Witch Project." But even if your film doesn't break box offices records, you still need to find ways to hang onto your integrity and your soul.

Did things change for you after *The Blair Witch Project* came out?

DAN MYRICK: Things did change, dramatically. People all of a sudden want to do business with you and they want make movies with you, and you didn't know them from Adam the day before.

With that kind of notoriety, it's real easy to lose your perspective on this business and on this industry because of the success and how big it became. And it was good for us to remind each other where we were just a few months prior to *Blair Witch* hitting it big.

You have to take it all with a grain of salt. You really have to be happy and excited that you've reached the level of success that you've always dreamt about; but at the same time, remembering why you got into this business and remembering the kind of movies you wanted to make is very important as well. Because it's really easy to go down that road, where all of a sudden people are sending you scripts and they want to pay you a lot of money to go do bad movies, just because they want to throw your name up on something.

For me, it's about common sense. We were offered several different movies, like *Exorcist 4*. I've forgotten the names of most of them. For better or worse -- myself in particular -- there's just a great reward in doing something that not everyone else is out doing.

It's too hard of a business, it's too hard of a process to go through and put your family through and put your wife through, if it isn't something you really believe in. There's nothing worse, I think, than seeing a filmmaker who's just miserable, with a lot of money at stake, having to take on a job or take on a film that they're really not passionate about, just to pay their huge mortgage.

There's a certain level of freedom that keeping things in perspective can give you. You can go into a meeting and say "No" if you don't believe in the project.

And I like having that freedom, I like having that autonomy.

FAST, CHEAP AND UNDER CONTROL: LESSONS LEARNED FROM THE GREATEST LOW-BUDGET MOVIES OF ALL TIME

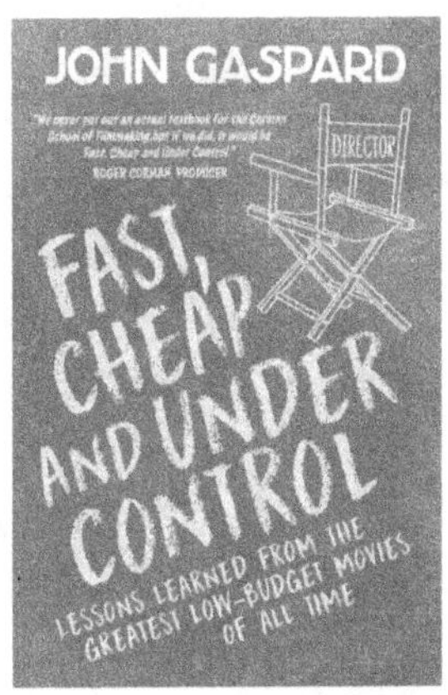

Learn the tricks and pitfalls of low-budget filmmaking from 33 successful independent films and the filmmakers who created them. Includes never before published interviews with low-budget mavericks such as Steven Soderbergh, Roger Corman, Jon Favreau, Henry Jaglom, and many more.

"We never put out an actual textbook for the Corman School of Filmmaking, but if we did, it would be *Fast, Cheap and Under Control.*"

Roger Corman, Producer

"This terrific little book explains how to make every penny count on the often-arduous journey from script to screen."

John Carpenter, Director, *Halloween, Starman, Escape from New York*

"A helpful and funny guide for beginners and professionals alike."

Jonathan Demme, Director, *Silence of the Lambs*

"This book is as good as film school, and a lot less expensive. It's required reading in Tromaville."

Lloyd Kaufman, President, Troma Entertainment, Creator, *Toxic Avenger*

"I wish I'd read this book before I made *Re-Animator.*"

Stuart Gordon, director, *Re-Animator*

GET YOUR FREE ELI MARKS
SHORT STORY BUNDLE

The Eli Marks Short Mystery Bundle
"The Invisible Assistant" & "The Last Customer"
Two short-story cozy mysteries in one!

"You will just LOVE these books."– VANISH Magazine

The Invisible Assistant

There's no question it was murder. But who killed whom?

What begins as a typical corporate event for magician Eli Marks turns into a twisted mystery when he is called to the site of a recent murder/suicide. Confronted by the details of the grisly crime scene,

Eli must sort through the post-mortem clues - and the bickering of the officials as well as a poorly-timed allergy attack - to determine just who murdered whom.

The Last Customer

The request was a first for Eli Marks: "Can you help me make my tuba disappear?"

Magician (and magic shop owner) Eli Marks is confronted with this odd demand just before he is about to close up shop for the day. Over the next few tense minutes, he finds a solution to that question which also, fortunately, puts him the positive side of what turns out to be a life-or-death situation.

Go to www.elimarksmysteries.com

THE AMBITIOUS CARD

AN ELI MARKS MYSTERY

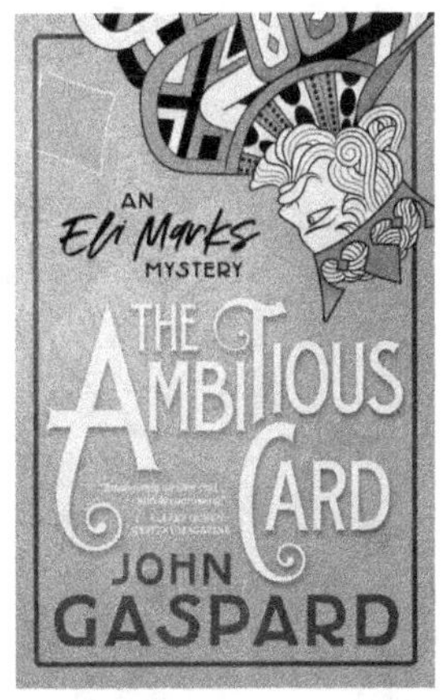

THE AMBITIOUS CARD
An Eli Marks Mystery (#1)
The life of a magician isn't all kiddie shows and card tricks.
Sometimes it's murder. Especially when magician Eli Marks very
publicly debunks a famed psychic, and said psychic ends up dead.
The evidence, including a bloody King of Diamonds playing card
(one from Eli's own Ambitious Card routine), directs the police right
to Eli.

As more psychics are slain, and more King cards rise to the top, Eli can't escape suspicion. Things get really complicated when romance blooms with a beautiful psychic, and Eli discovers she's the next target for murder, and he's scheduled to die with her. Now Eli must use every trick he knows to keep them both alive and reveal the true killer.

Grab this fun and funny mystery today!
https://www.elimarksmysteries.com

ACTING CAN BE MURDER

A COMO LAKE PLAYERS MYSTERY
(BOOK ONE)

The Phrase "Dying On Stage"
Takes on a Whole New Meaning

After fleeing a failed relationship in New York, actress Leah Sexton finds herself as the new Executive Director of the Como Lake Players–a small community theater nestled in a sleepy St. Paul neighborhood. The initial calm of this new position is shattered immediately when a local critic–who had just panned the theater's latest production–is found murdered on the show's set.

On the heels of this grisly discovery, the show's lead actress tumbles down a flight of stairs–or was she pushed? In order to keep the show running and the theater afloat, Leah offers to step into the leading role. The arrival of her ex-boyfriend amid anonymous threats against her and the show require Leah to act as if her life depends on it. Because it does.

(Previously released under the pen name Bobbie Raymond)

Grab this funny, twisty mystery today!
https://www.albertsbridgebooks.com

THE SWORD & MR. STONE

A Wild Modern-Day Quest for King Arthur's Magical Sword, Excalibur!

Insurance adjuster Edward Stone's quiet life is completely upset when he's drawn into a wild search for King Arthur's fabled lost sword, Excalibur.

From the towering monuments of Stonehenge to the dark mists of Loch Ness, Stone finds himself battling evil forces intent upon possessing this long-lost treasure.

It's only when he embraces the magical nature of the legend that's Stone is finally able to harness the epic forces behind Excalibur, the Sword of Power.

"A hero is no braver than an ordinary man, but he is brave five minutes longer." — Ralph Waldo Emerson

Grab this funny, gripping adventure today!
https://www.albertsbridgebooks.com

THE GREYHOUND OF THE BASKERVILLES

A new take on the Arthur Conan Doyle's classic mystery, "The Hound of the Baskervilles."

Think you know this story? Well, you haven't experienced it until you've read it through the eyes of Sherlock's pet dog.

It's the classic tale, now narrated by a dog. A greyhound, in fact, named Septimus.

Holmes and Watson ... and Septimus ... are called to the Baskerville
estate to protect the new Baron and see if there is any truth to the
legend of the hound of the Baskervilles. It's a dog-meet-dog mystery
as Septimus sniffs out the clues, detects the red herrings and goes
head-to-head with the monsterous creature which is haunting the
moors.
It's the classic you love ... but now it's a slightly different tail!

"A delightful tale, familiar and yet filled with surprises."

Grab it now!
★★★★★
https://www.albertsbridgebooks.com

THE RIPPEROLOGISTS

"Who are you?"

"For tonight, you can call me Jack. Mind if I come in?"

"Fascinating, couldn't put it down!"

Nunes, Amazon.com (verified purchase)

★★★★★

When a copycat serial killer begins recreating Jack the Ripper's 1888 murder spree, two competing experts are forced to work together to stop him.

What they don't understand is that his murderous spree is far more personal than either of them ever suspected.

Grab this electrifying race-against-time mystery/thriller today!

https://www.elimarksmysteries.com

★★★★★

BOOKS BY JOHN GASPARD

The Como Lake Players Mysteries
ACTING CAN BE MURDER
DYING TO AUDITION
REHEARSED TO DEATH

The Eli Marks Mystery Series
THE AMBITIOUS CARD (#1)
THE BULLET CATCH (#2)
THE MISER'S DREAM (#3)
THE LINKING RINGS (#4)
THE FLOATING LIGHT BULB (#5)
THE ZOMBIE BALL (#6)
THE MAGIC SQUARE (#7)
THE SELF-WORKING TRICK (#8)

Stand-Alone Novels
THE SWORD & MR. STONE
A CHRISTMAS CARL
THE GREYHOUND OF THE BASKERVILLES
THE RIPPEROLOGISTS

Filmmaking Books
FAST, CHEAP AND UNDER CONTROL
FAST, CHEAP AND WRITTEN THAT WAY
TELL THEM IT'S A DREAM SEQUENCE
WOMEN MAKE MOVIES

ABOUT THE AUTHOR

John is author of the Eli Marks mystery series as well as four other stand-alone novels, *"The Sword & Mr. Stone," "A Christmas Carl," " The Greyhound of the Baskervilles"* and *"The Ripperologists."*

He also writes the *Como Lake Players* mystery series.

In real life, John's not a magician, but he has directed six low-budget features that cost very little and made even less—that's no small trick.

He's also written books on the subject of low-budget filmmaking. Ironically, they've made more than the films. Those books (*"Fast, Cheap and Under Control"* and *"Fast, Cheap and Written That Way"*) are available in eBook, Paperback and audiobook formats.

John lives in Minnesota and shares his home with his lovely wife, several dogs, a few cats and a handful of pet allergies.

Find out more at: https://www.albertsbridgebooks.com and https://www.elimarksmysteries.com.

facebook.com/JohnGaspardAuthorPage

twitter.com/johngaspard

instagram.com/johngaspard

bookbub.com/authors/john-gaspard